This Notebook Belongs To

____

www.ingramcontent.com/pod-product-compliance
Lightning Source LLC
LaVergne TN
LVHW061941070526
838199LV00060B/3906